Blooms on bedrock

BY MEA KAEMMERLEN

The story of A Mountain Garden

PHOTOGRAPHS: CRAIG GILBORN

THE ADIRONDACK MUSEUM   BLUE MOUNTAIN LAKE   NEW YORK

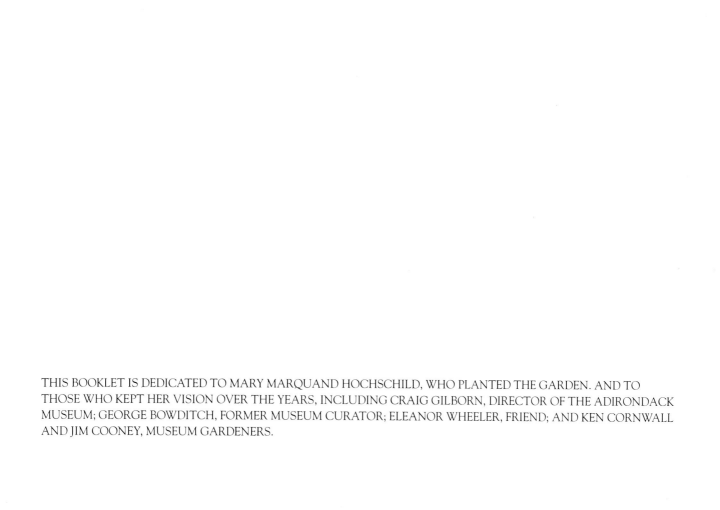

THIS BOOKLET IS DEDICATED TO MARY MARQUAND HOCHSCHILD, WHO PLANTED THE GARDEN. AND TO THOSE WHO KEPT HER VISION OVER THE YEARS, INCLUDING CRAIG GILBORN, DIRECTOR OF THE ADIRONDACK MUSEUM; GEORGE BOWDITCH, FORMER MUSEUM CURATOR; ELEANOR WHEELER, FRIEND; AND KEN CORNWALL AND JIM COONEY, MUSEUM GARDENERS.

Editor: Alice Wolf Gilborn

Principal Photography: Craig Gilborn

Additional Photography: Peter Lemon, Karen Halverson

Library of Congress Catalogue Card Number: 92-70781

International Standard Book Number: 0910020-41-8

Designed by Lemon and Lemon, Long Lake, New York
Typeset in Goudy Old Style by Partners Composition,
    Utica, New York
Printed by Brodock Press, Inc., Utica, New York
Published by the Adirondack Museum of the Adirondack
    Historical Association

Contents

6   Apology

8   A Glimpse of the Lake

10   The Setting of a North Country Garden

12   The Weaver of the Gardens

14   Planting on the Mountain

18   A Tapestry of Flowers

28   A View Framed in Marigolds

34   Giving Shrubs Their Due

40   Trees and Neighbors

46   Nature On Her Own Terms

54   The Reverend Bull's Garden

58   Garden Runaways and Settlers

62   End Note: A Year on the Mountain

68   Tributes

Apology

There was once a father who worked very hard during the week and tended lovingly to his family, house, and garden on the weekends. One warm Saturday, he went to a tree nursery, bought a beautiful magnolia sapling, carted it home, and planted it. On Monday, when his six-year-old daughter came home from school, she noticed the new tree in the middle of the lawn. Examining the rough grey bark, she saw that, underneath, the trunk was clean and shiny. She decided to continue her father's work and struggled to peel off the knobby bark, eventually exposing a column of smooth, damp, naked wood.

When her father came home, she proudly showed him the work she had done. He stared at the little tree and its scattered bark and kept repeating, "You did that? How could you do that?" The tree died a week later.

That unhappy man was my father. The girl was me.

With such an ignominious beginning, why am I writing a booklet on the plantings of the Adirondack Museum? For years the museum has graciously asked me, in my semiprofessional capacity as horticulturist (or is it "morticulturist"?) to come by to observe the plantings, suggest new ones, salvage old ones, and generally comment on the state of the museum campus. Over the years, several very good gardeners have seen to the care, feeding, and well-being of the gardens and plants at the museum, and whatever I have to say about the plants can be elaborated twenty-fold by any one of them. My experience (beyond childhood) is based on training at the New York Botanical Garden's School of Horticulture and ten subsequent years of work with plants in New York City at the New York Botanical Garden and the Horticultural Society of New York and as a freelance landscaper.

A brief word on plant nomenclature. Before humans arrived to give them names, plants grew very well indeed. With the appearance of human beings came the passionate addiction for imposing order on the world. Consequently, plants, with all other things, were given names to differentiate them and indicate to which group of plants they belonged. They are now continually being classified, named, reclassified, and renamed. Depending on who discovered the plant, how it was categorized, and which system of botanical nomenclature (Latinized names) was used, a plant might have several official names. Their common names, of course, are even more variable, each plant called something different by the local residents of a particular valley or mountain or river plain. Plant breeders and nurseries often add their own version. In this booklet, in an effort to be simple and clear, I have generally used the common names of plants as they are known in the Adirondacks and the botanical names as they appear in the major horticultural reference encyclopedia, *Hortus Third*,

put out by the staff of the L. H. Bailey Hortorium at Cornell University and published by Macmillan Publishing Company.

A glimpse of the lake

Thirty-five years ago a garden was planted in the heart of the Adirondacks. Since then, like many gardens, it has been dug up, replanted, enlarged, redesigned, reduced, nurtured, lamented, admired. It sits on ten acres of land, 220 feet above the water of Blue Mountain Lake, and 1,750 feet below the crest of Blue Mountain. Situated on the grounds of the Adirondack Museum, it weaves around old hotels, rustic gazebos, glacial outcroppings, exhibition halls, asphalt pathways, and a duck and boat pond. For the annual museum audience of 100,000, the garden is itself an exhibit of the plants that populate the North Country—the trees, shrubs, and flowers of the murky bogs, rugged mountainsides, and open woodlands that surround the museum. In a way, the garden is a tame canary in the midst of a wild flock of chickadees, a familiar pet among its cousins in the wild.

Inside the Adirondack Museum's Main Building, one of 22 stops and perhaps the only "museumy" building along the visitor path, are several dioramas—three-dimensional lifelike scenes, set deep into the exhibit walls. One depicts loggers in a bunkhouse in an Adirondack logging camp ("they ate, at one sitting, four hundred eggs, three whole hams, and innumerable loaves of bread"); another, a field of hay being harvested as seen through the mud-spattered panes of a farmhouse kitchen window. Visitors raise audiophones to their ears to hear the commentary and peer through the glass frame, letting their imaginations fill in the action of the scene. Set

in a diorama frame on the end wall, complete with audiophone, is a typical Adirondack lake scene, with serene islands, a well-defined shoreline, and distant, misty mountains. This diorama, however, is a fake. The water and hills have not been sculpted by a specialist in New York City. This is actually a clear glass window overlooking Blue Mountain Lake, its islands, and distant mountains. Visitors inevitably chuckle when they realize they have been "taken in." They have just had their first glimpse of *the real thing*.

The museum is like this room in the Main Building. It is packed with historical artifacts, replicas, and documentation, the sum of which, for a typical four-hour visitor, equals an eye-opening glimpse into *the real thing*.

The Adirondack Museum was founded by Harold K. Hochschild, a New Yorker who spent 86 of his 88 summers in Blue Mountain Lake. His love of this gentle and remote part of the Adirondacks cut through his business and social life in New York City. For thirty years, he worked on a history of the Blue Mountain Lake area called *Township 34*, published in 1952. In 1948, he and William Wessels, proprietor of a summer hotel called the Blue Mountain House, formed the Adirondack Historical Association. Soon

a museum to document the history of the Adirondacks was being planned, and it opened in 1957 with a trove of North Country treasures rounded up from attics, boat houses, hotels, rustic camps, and a hermit's home. Since then, it has expanded in land and in exhibits. Its newest exhibits have focused on the critical role the environment has had in shaping the Adirondacks.

Left: Gazanias on the museum View Deck.
Above: The museum from 5,000 feet.
Right: Young mountain ash.

The setting of a north country garden

The Adirondack region, about seven million acres of wild country stretching from Saratoga Springs to near Canada, was once under a massive sea called the Grenville Sea. A billion years ago, the bottom of that sea erupted into archipelagos of island volcanos, five and six miles high, higher than the present Himalayan peaks. Five hundred million years passed and the mountains were reduced to hills by the erosion of sea water. A million years ago, when one-celled creatures were swimming about, the earth cooled and huge sheets of ice formed until mile-high glaciers covered the mountains, valleys, and streams. Their size and watery runoff played havoc with the land, creating wide rivers, gouging out valleys, damming streams, shearing off tops of mountains, until smooth bald granite held firm under the colossal weight of ice and snow. Finally, ten thousand years ago, the last glacier melted into thousands of miles of brooks and streams that coursed through the cracked and creviced land.

The terrain that is now Blue Mountain Lake, home of the Adirondack Museum, bore it all: the wetness of sweeping seas and the cold of smothering ice. On the museum grounds, evidence of the past billion years can be seen in rock outcroppings, erratics (rocks from other formations carried here by glaciers), primitive mosses, ferns, pines, and, more recently, chipmunks, bears, and humans.

In 1867, Miles Talcott Merwin of Durham, Connecticut, bought over 11,000 acres in the

Adirondacks, including what is now the village of Blue Mountain Lake. He sent his son, Miles Tyler Merwin, to investigate the purchase, and, after studying the lumbering trade in Glens Falls, Tyler set up a sawmill operation just below the museum's present location. On the western slope of Blue Mountain, overlooking the lake, he put up his barn and cabin. As early photographs attest, the land was "cleared," meaning that the forest was beaten back, leaving a cemetery of stumps to cover the slope.

In the summer of 1874, the future governor of Connecticut, Vincent Coffin, and his son, Seward, found themselves in Blue Mountain Lake with no place to stay. Tyler Merwin gave them supper and put them in the haymow of his barn. Coffin was enthralled with the site and asked the lumberman if he could build a cabin. Merwin agreed and, realizing that ready cash was to be had by providing room and board, built Blue Mountain House, where guests could stay for seven dollars a week. His was among a number of fashionable Blue Mountain Lake hotels (one of which boasted Edison electric light bulbs in every room and a two-story outhouse connected to both floors of the hotel). In 1876, Merwin erected an additional log cabin for guests. In the 1950s, the hotel was demolished to make way for the Adirondack Museum, but, after 115 years, the hewn log house from 1876 still overlooks the lake from its original spot.

Few of the original plants remain. In the late 1980s, several ancient infirm maples around the old log hotel were removed, and, about five years ago, a gnarled elderberry bush, one that probably had provided jelly for the hotel's breakfast table, died. The grassy slopes around the hotel were cut with a scythe and a road ran downhill to the lake. Such dust, however, was kicked up by cars with their admiring passengers that William Wessels, who bought the hotel from Merwin in 1935, blocked off the road and built a large parking area in the back for visitors.

The daylily, an important member of the museum's old guard. Above: Foxglove, or digitalis, grows on Merwin Hill.

The weaver of the gardens

Mary Hochschild was the weaver of the gardens of the Adirondack Museum. Just as the museum's staff conceived and implemented the exhibits that told of life, work, and leisure in the Adirondacks, Mary, wife of the museum's founder Harold K. Hochschild, created their setting—beautiful grounds in which she worked for years, constructing beds, choosing plants, and seeing to their care and nurture. Many of her original plantings delight museum visitors to this day, and large redwood tubs of red geraniums and lavender petunias are planted yearly according to the tradition she started thirty years ago. Her dedication was unflagging from the time the museum was built until her death seventeen years later.

At Mary's memorial service in 1974, former museum curator George Bowditch reflected: "Spring to me at the Adirondack Museum was heralded not so much by the passage of birds north nor the coming of green to the campus as by the arrival of Mary—her chief concern to find what had survived the winter's worst and to see to the repair of damages and the development of new plantings. Old friends were greeted anew, tender survivors were given a good scratching of encouragement around their roots, and the sick and the maimed had prescriptions written for their improvement. . . ."

Mary Hochschild grew up loving plants. Her childhood was spent on a Princeton, New Jersey, estate which had first been tended by "a remarkable gardener named Petrey" from the great English estate, Chatsworth, and then by a number of passionate and sometimes eccentric owners. Now a public park, its shrubs and trees reflect the height of 19th-century plant exploration: twelve species of magnolias, Algerian and Spanish firs, a dawn redwood (*Metasequoia glyptostroboides*). The latter was thought extinct until discovered in China in 1944 and carefully grown from a handful of seeds at Harvard's Arnold Arboretum.

While living in Princeton, Mary Hochschild spent her summers in Keene Valley, northeast of Blue Mountain Lake, where she learned the challenge of gardening in the North Country. She knew that here, more than elsewhere, the "ten-dollar hole" was essential to the well-being of the "five-dollar plant." A plant could do wonderfully if given the right start. She knew that the museum was built on bedrock, and that, for a cluster of poplars to survive, six feet of topsoil was needed. For lilies and peonies to thrive, two feet of topsoil and excellent drainage was critical. Workers accustomed to thin mountainous soils still speak admiringly of the loads of topsoil trucked in to Blue Mountain Lake. Needless to say, Mary was a familiar sight during the construction of the museum.

It is a tribute to Mary Hochschild's work and judgment that for over 35 years the same plants, or perhaps their great-grandchildren, have proved to be the stalwart stars of today's museum beds and of the Cutting Garden, which is harvested weekly for flower arrangements in the exhibit areas. Her choices were excellent, and her ten-dollar holes have paid off a hundred-fold. Her vision continues today as a guide to all who work on the museum grounds: to show the world that, if given a chance, plants do very well deep in the Adirondacks.

Above: Peonies and coral bells.

Left: Redwood tubs with petunias, a tradition started by Mary Hochschild thirty years ago.

Right: The museum Cutting Garden with Members Cottage behind.

Planting on the mountain

Surprisingly, Adirondack weather—early frosts, howling winter winds, and summer storms—nurtures a host of perennial flowers, flowers that return from their living roots year after year. Drooping and weak in more southern climates, the charming pink lupine, brilliant blue delphinium, and bright red cardinal flower flourish through the Adirondack summer. Several factors are at work here: cool nights which encourage root growth; clear nourishing air; a blanket of snow settling early and lifting late, protecting the dormant roots from crackling, dry frosts. With this heavy cover, even tender plants do well here: the large swamp plant, *Bergenia cordifolia*, which suffers severe browning after a Long Island winter, here leafs out fresh, green, and unblemished in early spring. The Oregon grape (*Mahonia aquifolium*), considered hardy only to Long Island, has thrived on the museum's hillside since the early part of this century when a summer cottage resident planted it in his garden. On the other hand, such garden staples as roses and rhododendrons struggle to survive. Given these unusual conditions, new plants for the museum are selected with care, but not without some risk to their well-being. This, of course, is what makes it fun.

Timing is as important as the choice of plant. The museum is open from the end of May to the middle of October. Azaleas often blossom not in April or May as promised by nursery catalogs but in July. Lilacs might flower in Albany on the first of May, but here they conveniently wait until the museum opens on Memorial Day. Visitors are often fooled by the unique Adirondack calendar. More than a few people have remarked, "That *looks* like mock-orange, but couldn't be—it's flowering a month late!"

In deference to the severe temperatures, planting and transplanting must be done early, no later than the end of September. No procrastinating until the leaves are raked, as in New Jersey or Connecticut. When frost settles into the ground, perhaps by mid-November, the new roots must be fully formed and in good working order to see the plant into the following spring.

The soil at the museum is good, having been custom-ordered by Mary Hochschild when the campus was first built and augmented later as necessary. Bedrock, however, is ubiquitous, and smooth grey granite erupts here and there from the earth. Garden beds must be built with great care to provide a "ten-dollar hole," and careful consideration must be given when a plant is moved so that its new location is deep enough for survival. In a wet summer, the soil's shallowness is not evident, but during dry spells, plants will suddenly wilt for lack of moisture.

The right location is critical not only for depth of soil but for the mounds of snow that fall from the roofs of the buildings. Shrubs and trees must be planted away from buildings or safely under the overhang, in which case they need constant watering during the summer, as the rain doesn't reach them. In some cases perennials which die back in winter are used in place of vulnerable shrubs in these locations.

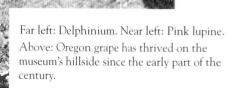

Far left: Delphinium. Near left: Pink lupine. Above: Oregon grape has thrived on the museum's hillside since the early part of the century.

A Dozen
of the Best

foxglove
bearded iris
Siberian iris
phlox
myrtle
hydrangeas
daylilies
heliopsis
astilbe
lilies (including Turk's-cap)
hosta
bush cinquefoil

Looking past a locust tree to
Boat Bubble Garden.

A tapestry of flowers

If the museum campus is viewed as a tapestry, its flower beds are an embroidery of blossoms along pathways, stone walls, and exhibit buildings. Some beds, such as the White Garden near the Boat Building, are built simply to be fanciful. In the tradition of great European gardens, this circular bed nurtures only white-blossoming plants, achieving a monochromatic tranquility of texture and form. An evening in a white garden is a special treat. With the darkening sky, white flowers can develop a sweet, pungent fragrance to draw in moths and other night-flying pollinators. (If you are ever invited to a "night-blooming cereus" party, don't hesitate. The huge flower buds of this leggy tropical cactus open only for one night and display their opulent white blossoms and strong sweet perfume until dawn. Champagne is usually served, though a case of beer suffices.)

In the White Garden, the balloon flower (*Platycodon grandiflorus*) is the main structural plant. It is a large clumpy mound carrying five-petaled white blossoms along the stalk. Before opening, the five petals are fused into what appears to be a tiny hot-air balloon. Early in the season, when the ground-covering potentilla and myrtle are in flower (the latter daring to show a blue blossom in the White Garden, but most of the season is a cover of discreet green), a two-foot circle of wire mesh is positioned around each balloon flower plant just bursting from the soil, in anticipation of its lusty growth.

Interspersed among the balloon flowers are tissue-petaled irises revealing their white blossoms in early July. Iris leaves—strong, pointed blades rising straight from the soil—offer good contrast to other more fluttery foliage in the garden. With them grow coral bells (*Heuchera sanguinea*), whose bells are here not coral but white, and *Veronica latifolia* 'Icicle,' its tiny flowers opening consecutively along each spiky stalk. Formerly, the Tartarian honeysuckle served as a backdrop to the garden, spewing forth white honeysuckle flowers in August (if something can withstand the tundra of the Tartars, it certainly can take the Adirondacks!). Now, in the wake of inevitable expansion projects at the museum over the years, peegee hydrangeas (*Hydrangea paniculata* 'Grandiflora'), whose common name is taken from its initials, have been planted

18

Left: Siberian iris in June. Above: A pathway near the Bubble Garden with baby's-breath, yarrow, iris and delphinium. Right: The balloon flower is the main structural plant in the White Garden near the Boat Building.

A tapestry of flowers

instead. The flowers of the peegee become slightly pink as they age, but this is allowed.

The Bubble Garden is another showy, purely indulgent bed and is named for the nearby 30-foot plastic protective dome, or "bubble," in which floats the racing sloop, *Water Witch*, from the St. Regis lakes (two hours north), its 25-foot mast casting a shadow over the bed by midday in the fall. The front of the raised triangular garden is edged with a handsome stone wall over which cascade two low plants, baby's-breath (*Gypsophila paniculata*) and creeping juniper (*Juniperus horizontalis* 'Blue Rug'). In a good year, the baby's-breath puts out from its green mat clouds of tiny white flowers catapulting over the cool grey stones. The juniper is actually a shrub, related to the common red cedar (*Juniperus virginiana*), inevitably the first tree to appear in abandoned fields. The creeping juniper, through nature and breeding, lies prostrate, with a spread of five feet and a height of only about four inches. This hunched deportment evolved, no doubt, as protection against the strong winds of its native Canadian habitat. Juniper berries are used to flavor gin.

The daylily and the phlox vie for the position of queen of the Bubble Garden. The word *phlox* comes from the Greek for "flame," and clusters of phlox (*Phlox paniculata*) with such varietal names as 'Fairy Petticoat,' 'Dodo,' 'Bright Eyes,' and 'Othello' flaunt their vibrant colors in the soft June breezes. Daylilies (several species of *Hemerocallis*) decorate the garden with fountains of long-bladed leaves and arching flower stalks, each stalk laden with fat buds ranging in color from light pink to dark orange (and never seeming to clash with each other). Each bud opens into a bell-shaped blossom for a single day, its dazzling color adequate compensation for its short life.

Other flowers in the Bubble Garden are bright blue cornflowers (*Centaurea montana*) and delphiniums; yellow yarrow and white shasta daisies; butterfly weed (*Asclepias tuberosa*), a bright orange

Far left: Peonies, Siberian iris and bearded iris.
Near left: Bee balm flowers in July and August.
Above: Daylilies flaunt their colors June through September.

A tapestry of flowers

native plant related to common milkweed; stonecrop (*Sedum spectabile*), with its round succulent leaves and pink flowers, full of bees in late August; Aaron's rod or Carolina lupine (*Thermopsis caroliniana*), an under-used plant with a tall spike of yellow pea-like flowers; and globe thistle (*Echinops ritro*), a midsummer round, blue bristling head of flowers (*echinops* is Greek for hedgehog). In late summer, the garden is awash with the yellow daisy-like flowers of heliopsis (*Heliopsis helianthoides*) which stand four to five feet and radiate the warmth of the sun. This is the plant of Adirondack farms and cottages, growing profusely wherever allowed. This particular one was tracked to a nearby abandoned farm cottage, a small portion anonymously uprooted, and planted in this bed. The peony (*Paeonia lactiflora*) has ornamented this garden for 35 years. Related to the lowly buttercup, which dutifully reflects itself on every child's chin, proving the universal love of butter, the peony has been cultivated since ancient times and, in June, throws open its petals to reveal a cluster of bright, pollen-laden stamens. Annual flowers and "volunteers" also make their way to this garden, changing its choreography every year.

If phlox and daylilies are queens of the Bubble Garden, the bearded iris is knight— sometimes even knight errant, because it is everywhere wielding its green, sword-like leaf blades and, in early summer, its showy multicolored plumage. Named for the messenger of the gods who used the rainbow for a path, the iris displays all colors of the prism in its blossoms. Each blossom has six petals of two different types: the *falls* (with the "beard") opening outward, and *standards* standing upright. The iris is propagated after it flowers in late June, the ginger-root-like tubers broken into pieces and replanted just below the surface of the soil. This gives the blades the remainder of the summer to nourish the newly independent tubers before winter's toll. The iris is a very generous plant, both with its colors and with its offspring, as each tuber can be broken into at least ten pieces to be given to friends and neighbors. The museum's irises grow in gardens for hundreds of miles around.

A cousin of the bearded iris is the Siberian iris (*Iris sibirica*), more modest in its flower but showy in its full clustered fountain of sharp thin leaves which lasts the whole summer and gives rise to blue, purple, and white flowers in mid-July. At the museum, the Siberian iris works well as a backdrop for smaller plants such as baby's-breath and clumped in the grass as a border along the path. It also grows in a wet area near the edge of the Boat Pond together with native cattails, which do surprisingly well.

In the spring of 1992 a watercourse was added to this natural wetland area which helps with the

Phlox.

aeration of the Pond and creates a stage for bog-and-water loving plants, including black cohosh (*cimicifuga racemosa*), pitcher-plants (*Sarracenia purpurea*), and Labrador-tea (*Ledum groenlandicum* Oeder).

The front of the Logging Building displays appropriate plantings: groves of hemlock, red spruce, white pine, and balsam, with a covering of blueberry bushes. Previous to the building's reconstruction, a series of four gardens lined the front of it, in full view of passers-by. Planned for flowering from June through September, the beds included daylilies; delphiniums; Aaron's rod; loosestrife; bee balm (*Monarda didyma* 'Croftway Pink'), a large scarlet flower that is irresistible to ruby-throated hummingbirds that inhabit the Adirondacks; globe thistle; and spiderworts (*Tradescantia x. Andersoniana*). The spiderwort's Latin name honors a 19th-century British father and son plant-hunting team, both named John Tradescant, who explored the eastern United States. They are buried with Admiral William Bligh of the *Bounty* at the Garden History Museum in London. This collection of perennials shared the bed with the amazingly successful shrub, cinquefoil (*Potentilla fruticosa*), flowering yellow or white during the entire summer. There is more on the cinquefoil in the chapter on shrubs. All of these plants have been moved to other gardens around the museum.

A garden flanks part of the Road and Rail Building, looking almost exactly as it did when planted in the late fifties. Mary Hochschild describes it in her 1974 booklet on museum plantings: "There is a bed holding pink Sweet Pepper (*Clethra alnifolia*), blue Amsonia (*Amsonia tabernaemontana*), and dwarf Baby's Breath (*Gypsophila repens*). Flanking these plants, which have thrived, are shrubs of Mock Orange (*Philadelphus coronarius*), also successful in that location."

The amsonia still thrives, a delightful but underused perennial, full, bushy, and topped with pale blue flowers in June and July. Behind the amsonia stand tall spires of sweet pepper, filled with tiny pink August flowers and surrounded by eager bees attracted to the sweet, strong fragrance. Into the grass in front of the bed jet puffy white clouds of baby's-breath. All these have done well for thirty years. About ten years ago, a clump of Siberian iris was added to fill out the bed and provide color in July. Nearby, in a semicircular bed backed by a stone wall, coral bells and astilbes color the light shade of an overhanging birch with a strong show of coral, white, and mauve flowers throughout the summer.

An important member of the museum's old guard is the lily, which adds a dramatic flare to several sites. Prominent flower beds on each side of the entrance to the museum's Main Building require

A tapestry of flowers

plants of stature and drama, but no flowering shrub can survive the winter ice and snow that slide from the roof onto this bed. The solution was the Turk's-cap lily (*Lilium superbum*) which now rise in numbers from a soft undulating bed of ferns, orange punctuation marks in a sea of green text. The lily bulbs are eight inches underground—safe from snow and ice during the winter—and rise to flower splendidly in July and August. Their unusual depth also makes them stronger: being four to five feet tall, they are prone to toppling from their own weight if shallowly planted. Lilies are not easy, but when they take to a certain site, they live for years. They need excellent drainage and prefer a ground cover, such as ferns, over their roots.

Related to the lily is the crocus, known for its spring blossoms, appearing too early for use at the museum. Less known but more valuable to the museum is the fall-flowering crocus (*Crocus nudiflorus*) which in October shoots up unexpectedly large purple and yellow flowers directly from the ground. By this time, the leaves, which grow all summer, have disappeared.

Ferns, especially the showy "osmundas," are used in the ornamental gardens as well as in the naturalized areas of the campus. A long row of three-foot royal ferns (*Osmunda regalis*) forms the backdrop to the pool in front of the Boat Building, and interrupted ferns (*O. claytoniana*) and cinnamon ferns (*O. cinnamomea*) are scattered here and there, sometimes appearing voluntarily. These two ferns are named for their unusual spore-bearing qualities; the cinnamon produces long stems bearing large cinnamon-sticklike clumps of spores, and the interrupted carries its spore cases intermittently along each green frond.

Hostas, natives of China and Japan, have emerged as staples in the museum gardens. Their wide handsome leaves, heavily ribbed and sometimes mottled green, white, and yellow, are used to define flower borders, to hide unsightly corners, and to add texture to colorful beds. When they flower in July, they send up tall, fluttery spikes of clustered purplish and white flowers.

A long row of three-foot royal ferns by the pool in front of the Boat Building.

May and June

myrtle
foxglove
sweet William
peonies
bleeding heart
coral bells
lungwort
iris
bergenia
goutweed
lupines
columbines
stitchwort
trout lilies
colt's-foot
forget-me-nots
trillium
Solomon's-seal
Solomon's plume
lady's-slippers
azaleas
mock-orange
bush cinquefoil
baby's-breath
yellowwood
black locusts
buttercups

A stone wall is a backdrop to a host of flowers; among them, marigolds, white and red coral bells and veronica.

A view framed in marigolds

Cantilevered from the lakeside corner of the museum's Road and Rail Building is the View Deck. Visitors—both dutiful sign-followers and free-spirited mavericks—are inevitably drawn onto the View Deck with its view of the lake, islands, and undulating horizon of mountains beyond.

Here is one of the museum's showiest displays of plants. On the L-shaped railing is a 200-foot parade of dazzling flowers wafting in the wind and shimmering in the sunlight. Twenty-four metal boxes, two feet wide and five feet long, are sunk into the chest-high railing, stretching around the distant corner of the building.

These crowd-pleasing flowers are annuals, plants that germinate from seed, grow, flower, set seed, and die in one season. Favorites are marigolds, impatiens, salvia, and begonias. Years of breeding have made their short expatriate lives possible, as these plants, hailing from tropical regions of Mexico, Thailand, and Brazil, are foreigners to the Adirondack climate. In spite of this, they are obedient to the photographs in nursery catalogs and burst forth with color and fragrance for the short

summer season, basking in the hot sunny days and cool nights of the mountains. High rollers of the plant world, they are prodigious feeders and are vulnerable to pests and diseases, thereby needing more attention than the sturdier garden plants. But they reward bountifully, blooming continually from early summer adolescence to frosty old age in the autumn.

Work on the flower boxes begins in February when Jim Cooney, the museum's chief gardener, orders about 500 annuals (16 per box, with some to spare) from a nursery. The choice is not easy and is based on wisdom gained with each passing year. Proven annuals for the View Deck are wax begonias, extravagant rose-like tuberous begonias, marigolds, lobelias, sweet alyssum, and dwarf dahlias. Gazanias cause great excitement with their large, extravagantly colored petals, but, like portulacas which were given up years ago, they willfully open *only* on sunny days. When the sky is overcast and drizzly—days of the museum's highest attendance—they are closed tight as a clothespin. Ageratum has done wonderfully over the years, with large, tight mounds of purple flowers so dense the green leaves can only struggle to get through. They tend, however, to fall apart toward the end of the season,

Left: Marigolds and Blue Mountain Lake from the View Deck.
Below: Begonias in planting box.

A view framed in marigolds

showing large empty holes, like cauliflowers with huge bites in the centers. Petunias are glorious in the boxes, but a gardener with 500 petunias would have to be committed solely to them since petunias require almost daily fertilizing, watering, pinching dead blossoms, and pruning.

The selection made, the nursery grows the seedlings to specification and hands them over to the museum. Though the museum opens in May, these plants cannot be set out until the danger of frost has passed, traditionally in early June (though, in fact, frosts can occur every month of the year). They are then planted, between other early summer chores of raking, cleaning, transplanting, and mulching. April may be the cruelest month, but June is the busiest. The soil in each box is rejuvenated with several pounds of good crumbly soil from the compost pile and a shot of slow-release fertilizer that lasts all summer. At planting, the small transplants are nourished with a half-strength dose of fertilizer, administered through a special measuring device attached to a long green hose which, at all times, hangs on the railing, coiled for action.

The flowers must be respectable by the July 4th weekend when tourists flock to the North Country in earnest, and the gardeners must perform several pinchings of the first flower buds to create bushier, fuller plants for the summer performance. They check them daily, clean them up weekly, and fertilize them every other week.

By August 1, the boxes look glorious, and even the vainest, most publicity-hungry plant receives sufficient attention. Every camera comes out ("Hey, someone forgot to load the film"), family portraits are taken ("Trust me, I'll send everyone a copy"), each flower gets its due ("In my garden last year, this yellow fuzzy one must have been a miniature").

Two perennials mingle with the annuals. The low-growing, sturdy *Teucrium chamaedrys*, with its modest blue flowers in September, tolerates children's bottoms, cameras, elbows doubling as tripods, purses, and bags better than most and so is planted in the boxes that give the best view of the lake. Also known as "poor man's boxwood," the *Teucrium* spends winters in the cutting garden, as root rot would set in if it remained on the View Deck. In the last two flower boxes, Jim Cooney has resorted to another perennial, a succulent, low-growing sedum, which grows freely at one of the old summer cottages on Merwin Hill. For some reason, no annual has ever done well in these last boxes.

In September, the annuals continue to be magnificent, but the gardeners now keep an eye on the weather. Any sign of a clear night with low temperatures means draping the boxes with a tarp, thus raising the temperature perhaps 15 degrees. A frost would kill many of the plants, and protection from the first frost usually allows the tropical colors to blaze almost until the museum closes in mid-October.

The view of the lake outshines the flowers—even "plant people" must concede this. The hillside below, covered with white daisies, blue asters, ash trees, beech trees, and breezy birches, slips quietly down to the water. The dazzling water stretches out to islands resembling proud ships afloat on the still water. In the distance, hills rise in the hazy air and give way to mountains.

Visitors have a rest here. There is nothing to read, to study, to examine, no numbers to follow. Here are flowers, bees, water, air, mountains, horizon. Visitors ease themselves onto the old rustic benches at the end of the deck, made of what looks like soft, smooth driftwood, and face the lake, enjoying the sun and the peace of the mountains.

For a hard-working gardener, the equivalent to the peace on the View Deck is leaning on your rake and looking out over the lawn. You see, you feel, you absorb, you relax, you take a little time out. Then the reverie is broken: you spot a large plantain weed growing in the middle of the impatiens and you move determinedly toward it.

Dahlias on the View Deck.

July

phlox
Siberian iris
lilies
bee balm
hosta
Aaron's rod
amsonia
delphinium
spiderwort
daisies
black-eyed Susans
yarrow
butterfly weed
mullein
daylilies
meadow rue
buttercups
orange hawkweed
meadow sweet
hydrangea
rosa rugosa
bush cinquefoil

Looking across pond to Marion River
Carry Pavilion with Logging Building
in distance.

Giving shrubs their due

In the United States, shrubs aren't given their due. They are usually limited to a "foundation planting," hugging the perimeter of a new house to camouflage cinder blocks and discolored cement. In Europe, especially in England, a shrub border is given the same care and applause as a perennial border and contains as many textures, forms, and colors.

The museum uses shrubs fully, and its collection is scattered over the grounds. The bush cinquefoil is the star. It is a member of the rose family and looks a bit like a large bushy wild strawberry vine. The museum's specimens are covered with yellow or white five-fingered flowers (thus the French name *cinquefoil* meaning "five fingers") throughout June, July, August, and even into September. The variety 'Katherine Dykes' is particularly full. Originally planted in several large mounds at the entrance to the museum grounds, they would be passed without comment by only the most hardened visitor. Due to museum construction, this original group was moved and replanted elsewhere. Interestingly (and frustratingly,

but gardeners are used to this), they have never done quite as well as they did in the original location. A group now planted in full sun along the path to the School House, which opened in 1989, is doing very well. For all its beauty, cinquefoil seems to be unappetizing to deer, which makes it particularly endearing to Adirondack gardeners.

Hydrangeas are as much a part of the museum as the boat or logging exhibits. For years, hills-of-snow (*Hydrangea arborescens* 'Grandiflora') stood as sentinels under the great roof of the Road and Rail Building, each large shrub softening a supporting buttress. In July and August, they produced great, flat heads of white flowers. Because they received no rainwater under the overhang and needed constant hand-watering, they were moved and now grace several sunny spots with huge white puffs each summer. The peegee hydrangea grows very well at the museum and is similar to the hills-of-snow, but it flowers about a month later in foot-long pyramidal clusters of white flowers. The peegee is a show-stopper for September visitors.

To turn the corner onto the View Deck in late June is to walk by a perfume factory. The source of the fragrance is not found in heart-shaped bottles bought by Fifth Avenue matrons, but in flat white

Left: Hydrangeas.

Above: Cinquefoil blooms through June, July and August
and even into September.

Giving shrubs their due

flowers surrounded by bees and butterflies in search of nectar. This is the mock-orange (*Philadelphus coronarius*), a large shrub named for its similarity in blossom and fragrance to the orange tree. Also commonly and confusingly called syringa, which is the botanical name for the lilac (no relation), it flowers for two weeks at the end of May in gardens further south. Here it is in its prime at the end of June and start of July, giving Fourth of July visitors the olfactory equivalent of a fireworks display.

As with the mock-orange or syringa, plant names can become quite muddled among botanists, horticulturists, and gardeners. Take, for example, a small neat shrub that, year after year, softens a portion of the harsh base of the Road and Rail Building. Its name is the dwarf highbush cranberry (*Viburnum trilobum var. nana*), which doesn't seem fair because there is nothing cranberry or highbush about it. It is a viburnum, and its cousin (*Viburnum trilobum*), living happily around the corner near the Cafeteria, is called highbush cranberry because its bright red berries resemble those of the true bog-hugging cranberry. I have seen neither flower nor berry on the small one, but it still sports the name.

A shrub that does live up to its name is the burning bush (*Euonymus alata* 'Compacta'), once planted as a hedge along the path to the Cafeteria. This hedge sat modestly, attracting hardly a murmur during June, July, and August, though if one looked closely, one could see the interesting peeling ridges of bark on the branches. As the weather cooled, the leaves became touched with red and soon formed a mound of dark glittering crimson, threatening the autumn supremacy of the sugar maple. Unfortunately, the deep crimson is now only history. An insidious attack of the scale insect, a dire enemy of all *Euonymus* species, weakened and killed the lovely hedge several years ago. A row of blueberries has cooled the spot considerably.

The North Country is not a place for rhododendrons and azaleas, though some manage, year after year, to struggle into spring. Many years ago, Mary Hochschild was given three azaleas by two New Jersey garden clubs. She probably did not have the heart to tell the members that this was rough country for those shrubs that served so many purposes in their own gardens further south. She planted them in a sheltered spot at the museum, and since then they have been nursed through the winters with yards of burlap and makeshift plywood teepees. What flower buds survive the winter finally dare to open as late as July. Recently several native deciduous pinkster azaleas (*Rhododendron periclymenoides* also known as *R. nudiflorum*), hardier than the evergreen varieties, were planted on the wooded Merwin Hill, and they blossom deep pink in the spring.

Experimental also is a non-native deciduous Exbury azalea named 'Aurora,' which time will have to judge.

Neither are roses meant for the North Country, but the sturdy *Rosa rugosa* proves the exception. The large rounded shrubs dot the path to the School House exhibit, displaying their fat red fruits—the rose hips used in tea and soup—in the fall.

On Merwin Hill are many native shrubs, both planted and growing naturally. A lovely native that is finding a sunny spot at the foot of the hill is meadowsweet (*Spiraea latifolia*), resident of wet, marshy areas, carrying tall pink spires in midsummer. Several native viburnums, arrowwood (*Viburnum dentatum*) and witch-hobble (*V. alnifolium*), grow here, familiar to hikers throughout the Adirondacks. Not easily transplanted, they will thrive once they have settled in. Three specimens of a native deciduous holly called winterberry (*Ilex verticillata*) grow contentedly in a shady spot but produce no berries in the fall. Because the male and female holly flowers grow on separate plants, there is speculation that all three shrubs are female, though the nursery swore there was a male among them. For majestic red-berried English hollies, one usually buys a small inconspicuous male holly called something like 'Little Bull' to do the job, but I doubt he would work for the winterberry.

Highbush cranberry flowers in June above, berries in August below.

August

balloon flowers
lilies
phlox
shasta daisies
astilbe
globe thistle
lamb's-ears
virgin's bower
daylilies
Turk's-cap lily
chicory
turtle-heads
bush cinquefoil
hydrangea 'Hills of Snow'
roses

A small grove of balsam poplars
on the bank of the Boat Pond.

Trees and neighbors

The mayor of Tupper Lake, just north of Blue Mountain Lake, was once asked for the population of his town. "Mostly spruce and hemlock," he answered. This is the North Country. Its people, mountains, villages, and lakes notwithstanding, the Adirondacks is essentially forest.

Walking into a forest is like walking into a crowd of strangers. The trees are at first equally unknown and strange. After a while, however, they emerge as individuals—some elegantly dressed, some modest, some friendly, some forbidding.

At the museum, these individuals are treated with respect. Native trees, such as cedars and white pines, shade the pathways between exhibits and are labeled with their common and botanical names. Here and there are exotic (a botanist's word for "non-native") trees, planted by Mary Hochschild and subsequent gardeners. These foreigners do not take well to the climate.

Of Adirondack conifers—evergreens bearing cones and needles—the museum has a fine display. The balsam (*Abies balsamea*) is perhaps the best

known, and, for many visitors, a whiff of balsam needles brings visions of mountains, streams, a roaring fire, and Christmas. For a dollar or so, this vision is available in local gift shops in the form of a small balsam-filled pillow. With the red spruce, the balsam tree dominates terrain above 2,500 feet to timberline. Above timberline grow only alpine plants.

The northern white cedar (*Thuja occidentalis*), another museum regular, offers the best trivia question for an Adirondack-lake crowd. Along the shore, where cedar proliferates, a sharp line, about five feet above the water, defines where all branches begin—nothing grows below that. The line is uniform around the lake's shoreline and islands. Why? It apparently has nothing to do with ice, water, or natural growth. It is the "browse line" made by deer walking onto the frozen lake and eating the cedar branches as high as possible. The needles are flat and palm-like, and the trunk looks as though a pair of giant hands took hold of each end and rung it slightly, twisting the bark like a barber's pole. The cedar plays many roles at the museum. It is prized in rustic furniture and other rustic structures, many of the museum's pieces being made of it. The gate to Merwin Hill, the Environmental Pavilion, and the

Near left: Stately sugar maple in October.

Far left: Aerial view of the museum,
Blue Mountain beyond.

Above: A mix of tamarack,
maple and poplar trees.

Trees and neighbors

Moodie Cottage all contain cedar, while the two-holer outhouse and gazebo have in their construction bark and slabs from native spruce.

The stretch along the Logging Building is ornamented with groves of the major timbers of the Adirondacks: white pine (*Pinus strobus*), hemlock (*Tsuga canadensis*), white spruce (*Picea glauca*), and balsam (*Abies balsamea*). In the uncut virgin forest of two centuries ago, 150-foot white pines stood abundantly, an irresistible target for white men who used them as ship masts and lumber. Hemlock was prized for the tannin in its bark, used to tan leather. Spruce and balsam were also used in construction of all types. The museum displays two white-pine columns, 27 inches in diameter, in front of the Main Building; and in a virtuoso performance, the Carry Pavilion, designed by architect Thomas Chapin and built in 1990 on the Boat Pond, has 28 supporting white-pine columns, some with Adirondack capitals.

Perhaps the most interesting conifer is the tamarack or larch (*Larix laricina*). In anticipation of fall, this 60-foot tree turns a golden-yellow, glowing against its dark conifer cousins. Then, like any maple or birch, it sheds every one of its long, soft needles to stand bare all winter. In spring, it comes to life, producing delicate tufts of pale green needles and pink "flowers," inspiring its French-Canadian name *epinette rouge*. It likes bogs, but is content in drier places. The grove of tamaracks by the museum's Mining Building is a year-round exhibit of changing color and texture.

Many old sugar maples (*Acer saccharum*) from the time of the 1874 Blue Mountain House inhabit the museum grounds. Coarse, weathered, the bark alive with gnarled growths, ridges, insects, and the drilling of generations of woodpeckers, these sugar maples manage, every spring, to release a lush canopy of green and, every September, to flame up crimson and orange in protest of the coming winter. A tree company comes to the museum to feed and prune the maples and cable together their weak branches, but this is at best a rearguard action: three old trees were recently cut down and reduced to firewood.

The white birch (*Betula papyrifera*) is a dapper young dandy—no modesty here. A fine specimen throws a canopy of light shade over a semicircular garden near the View Deck, its young branches shining burnt-gold and its trunk dazzling white. The toothed triangular leaves quiver with the slightest breeze, and the long fuzzy catkins, the fruit of the birch, hang from its branches as springtime ornaments. Another white birch has been recently planted near the one-room School House. Standing singly is not natural to birches, which normally sprout in groves in sunny, newly opened spots in the forest. Damaging winter winds and pesty borers ensure high

maintenance and low longevity at the museum, but the white birch pays its dues with its handsomeness.

On the bank of the Boat Pond is a small grove of balsam poplars (*Populus balsamifera*), their grey trunks long and clean, and their leaves twirling silvery green high above. Fast growers, they are related to water-loving willows and thrive at the pond's edge. A white poplar (*Populus alba*) greets visitors in the parking lot as they enter the museum. Its spherical crown burgeons with round, toothed leaves that have surprisingly soft, woolly undersides.

Several members of the pea (legume) family grow on museum grounds. A Kentucky yellowwood (*Cladrastis lutea*), a native of the American southeast, is a surprising survivor of 35 years of Adirondack winters, its longevity due, no doubt, to its protected home in a corner of the Boat Building. Carrying long panicles of fragrant white flowers in June and dark brown pods in August, it is named for the yellow dye which comes from its heartwood. A pair of black locusts (*Robinia pseudoacacia*) near a pathway elicit exclamations of pleasure when visitors get a whiff of the perfume of their whitish flowers in June.

A favorite tree of mine is the mountain ash (*Sorbus americana*) which grows in the oddest places. Not competing well in the forest, it must find its own niche, sometimes in the ancient duff of the top of a huge flat boulder. Other times, a mountain ash will be as bold as any hemlock or maple, thriving in a garden by a busy highway. At the museum, several mountain ashes grow in the woods not far from the path, and, yearly, the underbrush is cleared to reveal the bright red clusters of berries and rows of small round leaves along each stem. Robins and cedar waxwings feast on these berries in October.

Some trees are significant by their absence from the museum grounds. Black spruces (*Picea mariana*), uncomfortable in the company of other spruces and common forest trees, inhabit the two least hospitable areas of the Adirondacks: bogs and mountain peaks. In a bog they might march along a ridge a few inches above the waterlogged sphagnum moss; and on peaks, above any other tree or shrub, they gather in miniature forests only a foot or two high, amidst the alpine flowers that grow above timberline.

Above: Cedar with April ice. Right: The tamarack, or larch, turns a golden yellow in fall.

September and October

autumn-flowering sedum
heliopsis
goldenrod
Turk's-cap lilies
sweet pepper
poor man's boxwood
doll's-eyes (seeds)
peegee hydrangeas
roses
autumn-flowering crocuses

Tobacco plants on the View Deck.

Nature on her own terms

In 1985, the museum's Merwin Hill was an exciting puzzle aesthetically, philosophically, botanically, horticulturally. Now, after a half-dozen thoughtful and challenging years, the two-acre slope serves many masters, retaining its integrity as only something possessed by nature can. Rising gently up the mountain above the museum's plateau, Merwin Hill is an exhibit created by curators, architects, gardeners, and, above all, nature.

In 1953, when the Adirondack Historical Association bought the land designated for the museum site, wide slivers of the adjacent hillside were owned by individuals—former summer residents—who, one by one, offered to sell. These pieces of land had been developed over the past century in the same way condos spring up around resorts today. In 1890, city folk came to stay at Miles Tyler Merwin's scenic Blue Mountain House, paid their seven dollars a week, and found they wanted a piece for themselves. Merwin sold small lots on the hillside above the hotel to people from Syracuse, Rochester, New York City, Baltimore. By the 1930s,

eight cottages stood on the hillside, sharing with the hotel such amenities as water piped from a distant spring house. Like the hotel, these camps, anchored to the hillside by pins drilled into bedrock, became small parcels of domestication within the dark wilds of the North Country.

By 1985, the museum had obtained all of these tiny plots and their neglected relics of former human habitation: several rustic cottages, a lone stone chimney, underground septic tanks, and a cement staircase leading nowhere. Abandoned, the hill was a tangle of scrubby weeds, spindly red maples, and a rich carpeting of myrtle growing wild. Propitiously, the Sierra Club Legal Defense Fund had just facilitated an out-of-court settlement, with the proceeds to be used for a nature/ecology exhibit at the Adirondack Museum. The "Merwin Hill project" was launched.

The museum had a number of issues to address: the restoration of two summer camps, the furnishing of one with rustic furniture, the construction of a native plant trail, and the presentation of ecological issues in a new pavilion. Work started in all four areas.

Botanically, the hillside was in cultural confusion. A few native wild flowers vied with

Left: The Environmental Pavilion on Merwin Hill.

Left: Roadside Garden with St. Johnswort, daylilies and mullein.

Above right: Solomon's plume. Right: Orange hawkweed with Queen Anne's lace in background.

Nature on her own terms

roadside weeds, goldenrods, and wild brambles that had sprung up in the sunlight of felled trees. Delightful native columbines appeared in May, but within weeks, pesky wild lettuce and wild oats hung over them ominously. The more unruly of the former summer residents' garden plants, bred in such exotic places as Tibet or Tunisia, had escaped their boundaries and spread across the hillside, accepted as equals by the native plants. It was chaotic and, moreover, it looked terrible. The prospect of creating a wild plant trail was daunting.

A switchback path, designed by landscape architect Lisa Chapin, was cut into the hillside, shaped like the letter "Z," the three lines linking important structures—first, a "zig" from the lower service road, across a drainage ditch and up a hundred feet to a cottage under restoration (built in 1900 by the Reverend Archibald Bull of Binghamton); then a "zag" of another hundred feet to a planned environmental pavilion; then a "zig," the same distance, up an overgrown service road leading to the Moodie Cottage. The retaining wall of the path was built with flat fieldstones from an old farm in Bennington, Vermont—Adirondack stone is too round and fractures too sharply to be part of a dry wall. This dry wall, which can accommodate nature's

freezing, heaving, and thawing, leans into the steep hill, supporting the three-foot-wide path, which is topped with stone dust and cinders and backfilled with crushed gravel from the old Tahawus mine northeast of Blue Mountain.

With the path finished, we considered how to interpret the hillside to museum visitors. Dozens of questions surfaced: Should we organize the trail like a textbook or leave it as a natural laboratory? Should we allow only native woodland plants to grow, removing those that had, over the years, adopted the hillside as home? Should we make it as attractive as possible, with the most appealing plants tidied and labeled for easy observation? Should we label everything? Or nothing? Or only plants in flower?

Our first conclusion was that purity is for angels and auditors and that the hillside should work as a museum exhibit, as honestly as nature would allow. The drainage ditch would become a brook, hosting cardinal flowers, marsh mallows, and ferns. We would create ecological niches along the path—two feet of duff (the spongy woodland floor, the result of years of disintegrating leaves and twigs) for woodland plants, a sunny, gritty spot for lakeside plants, and a damp area for mosses, ferns, and liverworts.

A wonderful, intense botanist (and railroad aficionado), Dr. Michael Kudish of Paul Smith's College in Paul Smiths, New York, inventoried the hill. With notebook and magnifying glass, he identified 151 botanical inhabitants. Ninety-six were

native to the region, and fifty-five were outsiders that had been planted or naturalized on the hillside. Of the trees, seven were conifers and eleven were hardwoods. We felt heartened by the diversity, but knew that we had a lot of work ahead—the six existing species of ferns were not neatly clumped along the path waiting for labels, and the pine was a spindly tyke, showing no sign of developing into a 150-foot giant of Adirondack fame. Several of the hardwoods, including the beech (*Fagus grandifolia*) and the striped and mountain maples (*Acer pensylvanicum* and *A. spicatum*), were welcome additions, as they were not planted on the main museum grounds.

The wild flowers were the most fun and rewarding. We created sites along the path by dragging in huge rotting logs and tree trunks, wheeling in barrows of woodland duff, and littering the slope with twigs, leaves, bark, and stones, all of which seemed quite bizarre to the regular grounds staff. It was a bit theatrical, but we couldn't resist adding artistic touches of whitened birch bark, though there was no birch tree in sight. We then scoured the undeveloped parts of the hillside and found a large assortment of plants which we transplanted to sites visible from the path. What we

didn't find, we ordered from nurseries or received as gifts from museum friends.

We put both common and unusual wild flowers along the trail with different degrees of success. Under the beech and striped maple saplings grow two native trilliums, painted trillium (*Trillium undulatum*) and stinking Benjamin (*T. erectum*), in flower when the museum opens in May. The first is pinkish, and the latter is reddish-mauve, a color which attracts fetid-meat-loving flies, its pollinators. The trout lilies (*Erythronium americanum*), appreciated by local residents as one of the first forest plants to flower in the spring, show their long shiny leaves, mottled green and brown, among the scattered leaves. The

Above: Shasta daisy. Right: Yarrow and baby's-breath.

Nature on her own terms

tiny-leaved, ground-hugging goldthread (*Coptis trifolia*) and wintergreen (*Pyrola chlorantha*), with its red berries, wind among the trout lilies. Several doll's-eyes (*Actaea pachypoda*) were planted a few feet back from the path, so that the white berries, each with a black dot, peer back at the gazing visitor in late August. Berries from these plants were scattered in the woods near the Cafeteria and are now spreading there. The "belle" of the hillside in June is one of the Adirondack orchids, the pink lady's-slipper (*Cypripedium acaule*), each five-inch stalk topped with a fragile Cinderella slipper. Among the many orchids that inhabit the North Country, this and the purple fringed orchid (*Habenaria fimbriata* or *H. psycodes var. grandiflora*) are the showiest, though so far the museum does not have the latter.

A sunny spot on a ledge beside the path, wet from continual runoff, is host to an unlikely mix: clouds of blue forget-me-nots (*Myosotis scorpioides*), a moisture-loving native of Eurasia but naturalized throughout the Adirondacks, and the bunchberry (*Cornus canadensis*), a ground-hugging relative of the dogwood tree bearing the familiar whorls of four ridged leaves and crimson berries in the fall. Turtle-heads (*Chelone glabra*), with their toothed leaves and pinkish reptile-shaped flowers, grow nearby.

Solomon's-seal (*Polygonatum pubescens*) and Solomon's plume (*Smilacina racemosa*, unjustly called *false* Solomon's-seal—it deserves an identity of its own), both with early delicate white flowers and fall berries (black and red respectively), grow together with blue-berried cohosh (*Caulophyllum thalictroides*) and red-berried Jack-in-the-pulpit (*Arisaema triphyllum*). Recently, the bluebead lily (*Clintonia borealis*) has overcome its shyness to form a shiny cluster of dark blue berries in mid-July. My favorite wild flower, which grows lavishly on the hillside, is meadow rue (*Thalictrum polygamum*), a tall, loosely branching plant with small round bluish leaves and puffy plumes of tiny white flowers. The autumn pods resemble bursts of green stars.

Jim Cooney has many success stories at the museum, and the colt's-foot tale ranks high. It seems that at one of the path's switchbacks, children were shortcutting by jumping off the retaining wall to the garden bed and path below, a danger to themselves, the wall, and the plants. In searching for a plant dense and large enough to discourage this, he tried a few native colt's-feet (*Tussilago farfara*) from his own garden. Today, this bed is dense with a mass of insistently large, heart-shaped (or colt-hoof-shaped) leaves and, in May and June, with dandelion-like flowers. Now no one thinks of jumping into or over this bed. Next to them is another relative of the dogwood, the shrubby native red osier (*Cornus stolonifera* or *C. sericea*), showing flat white flowers in

June and white berries in October.

Mosses, lichens, and liverworts are displayed around the Environmental Pavilion, a surprising site for these difficult-to-grow plants, but, thanks to the skill of the gardening crew, they thrive on thin soil laid over two feet of gravel backfill over bedrock. Tufts of red-topped lichen ("British soldiers") march in step with the lowly liverworts. Lichens are interesting because they are made up of individual algae and fungus plants living symbiotically. Moreover, they produce complicated chemical reactions which can slowly (over millenia) disintegrate rocks, providing a foothold for other plants. Ferns are also clumped around the Pavilion and have always been full of surprises. The elegant but difficult maidenhair (*Adiantum pedatum*) thrives, whereas the invasive bracken (*Pteridium aquilinum*), which we hesitated to plant because of its rampant growth, refuses to live through a season. Rock ferns (*Polypodium vulgare*) wind in and out of the rocks of the rough retaining wall around the Pavilion. In the forest, these ferns can form a green mantle over huge boulders, giving the impression the rock could use a haircut. Wood ferns, lady ferns, New York ferns, others intermingle freely, defying all but the experts to differentiate them. Club mosses, lowly descendents of giant plants that contributed significantly to our present-day coal and oil reserves, grow here with mixed success. Providing a midsummer backdrop of clouds of tiny white flowers is a massive wild clematis vine called virgin's-bower (*Clematis virginiana*).

In the Environmental Pavilion, a Victorian-style structure of southern pine, western fir, and hand-split white cedar, are displayed changing exhibits that explore such subjects as genetic diversity and forest management. Under construction is the Eco-Trail, which starts at the Moodie Camp above the Pavilion and ends at Minnow Pond, slightly less than a mile away. Easily traversed, it will give visitors a chance to learn about the dynamic relationship that exists between man and nature in the Adirondacks.

In a sunny spot at the base of the hillside, we put in a roadside flower display to feature flowers commonly seen along the Northway and smaller roads. Here daisies (*Chrysanthemum leucanthemum*), yarrow (*Achillea millefolium*), chicory (*Cichorium intybus*), black-eyed Susans (*Rudbeckia hirta*), and orange hawkweed (*Hieracium aurantiacum*) compete in a jumble of colors the summer long. Surprisingly, most of these plants are not native to the U.S., but have happily sown themselves across the highways of the New World.

The Roadside Garden features black-eyed Susans and other flowers commonly seen along the Northway and smaller Adirondack roads.

Above: Turk's-cap lily in front of Main Building.

Right: Bull Cottage view from alcove on Merwin Hill.

The Reverend Bull's garden

The summer residents of the cottages on the hillside above Blue Mountain House sought to bring some domesticity to their little patch of wilderness. Among the trunks and parcels they brought each summer were packets of seeds, baskets of petunias, and pots of parsley to ornament their porches and gardens.

Reports are that the Reverend Clarence Archibald Bull of Binghamton, the summer priest at Blue Mountain Lake's Episcopal Church from 1905 to 1943, was an avid gardener. When his 1901 hillside cottage was restored by the museum and opened to the public in 1988, the landscaping was revived as well. Below the cottage veranda was a most unusual plant, which indicated that this was probably the location of Father Bull's original garden. It was the Oregon grape, a shrub known to do well in the mild climates of Portland and Baltimore but unusual here. Its common name reflects the round green seed produced from its yellow flowers in June. The very fact that such a tender plant had hung on through decades of neglect mandated that we honor it. In clearing around the Oregon grape, we found a pattern of rocks stretching in an oval about fifteen feet long and ten feet wide. We repositioned these stones to outline the garden and dug in others for additional support against erosion.

In planting the garden, we had several special considerations. First, it is seen only from the veranda of the cottage, ten feet above, so the effect of the prettiest bleeding heart, with its small hanging flowers, or the fullest veronica, with its tall straight spike, is lost to the viewer. Spreading plants with generous flat flowers are the most effective. A second consideration was sunlight—the center of the garden captures the sun about eight hours a day, but the periphery, shaded by tall trees, gets only two or three hours. Third, just as humans go to expensive restaurants for a good dinner, the animals of the woods come to the garden for a gourmet meal. (Though the only "live act" at the museum should be the gardens, the museum does have nighttime visitors such as deer, raccoons, and an occasional bear.) On some mornings, paw and hoof prints of many sizes are evident in the garden and across the hillside. Bears do most of their damage slipping down the hillside, whereas deer stop for early morning brunch. Some of the eating habits of deer are perplexing. One day they dine only on blossoms, and the next, only on leaves. It is very disappointing to come by in the morning to see that the buds of an exquisite lily were neatly stripped the night before.

The most successful plants in the garden thus far are peonies. Surprisingly, bergenia and ligularia (*Ligularia sibirica*), both marsh plants not known for their hardiness, healthily spread out their large leaves for the viewer on the veranda above. Lambs'-ears (*Stachys lanata* or *S. byzantina*) and lungwort (*Pulmonaria officinalis*) show off their fuzzy white and spotted leaves respectively to good effect. Mounds of wild geranium (not the common annual, but a more delicate perennial) blaze with pink flowers in July.

At the entrance of the Bull Cottage, where construction obliterated plant life, we created another ornamental garden with a backdrop of hydrangea shrubs. A section of the bed is an old-fashioned herb garden, with comfrey, lavender, chives, sage, and tarragon. By August, all of these herbs are dwarfed by the huge rhubarb in the middle of the garden. Here, too, are some of the museum's few roses, miniature ones that do surprisingly well with some care. In the fall, they must be covered with balsam boughs; even so, they die back almost completely in the winter and must be cut back

severely in the spring. In return, by midsummer, they are generous with their delicate pink and red blossoms. The bed is bordered by a row of broad-leaved hostas which become very showy in July when they throw out tall stalks flowering white against the hydrangeas.

Above: Daylily.
Left: Hydrangeas and roses at the Bull Cottage.

The Bubble Garden is a showy, purely indulgent bed named for the nearby 30-foot plastic protective dome in which floats the racing sloop, *Water Witch*.

Garden runaways and settlers

For some plants, the Adirondack Museum is Ellis Island. They landed here with summer residents, were admitted onto the site, and have ventured some distance from their original garden boundaries. Survivors, they have become as prolific as any of the native plants and are making their own contribution to the grounds of the museum.

Two of the best are foxglove (*Digitalis purpurea*) and sweet William (*Dianthus barbatus*). These are the charm of the hillside during June and July when, by the hundreds, they rise out of the tangle of grasses and underbrush to paint the landscape pink, purple, and white. Foxglove has a stalk that stands two to five feet high and is covered with cheerful bell-like flowers from bottom to top. (It also produces a beneficial—and poisonous—substance which is used in the treatment of heart ailments.) Sweet William has a shorter flower stalk but sways its dense pink clusters in airy profusion. Both plants were probably brought here as garden plants and seeded themselves outside their boundaries.

As biennials, these two have short, interesting life cycles. The seed of the foxglove germinates in the spring and grows into a healthy rosette of leaves during the first year. The next spring, the flower stalk rises from the rosette, lined with tight green flower buds. From the flowers, seeds form, ripen, and scatter before the plant dies in autumn. Sweet William has a similar life span, with a more delicate earth-hugging rosette. How, you might ask, can there be so many flowers *each* year, not all leaves one year and all flowers the next, alternating year after year after year? As always in nature, there are no hard and fast rules, and sometimes a seed formed in August will germinate in September and shoot up a flower the following summer. The cycle is then started for the *alternate* alternating years. (This is probably as clear as what waterlilies grow in!)

Another Fortune 500 immigrant is *Vinca minor*, the common evergreen ground cover known as myrtle. Native to Europe, it now spreads a shiny dark green blanket over the hillside and, in spring, just when the museum is opening, it shows off an iridescent blue flower. At its best, myrtle prevents even the most invasive weeds from penetrating its carpet. However, where sunlight is increased by the falling of a tree or branch, goldenrods and wild oats easily get hold. A more subtle ground cover on the hillside is the Virginia creeper (*Parthenocissus quinquefolia*), which is used with great success by the museum as a climber to soften grey walls of some of the museum buildings. Here and there also, colorful spiky lupines are allowed to rise from the ground covers. The name *lupine*, from the Latin word *lupus* meaning "wolf," results from the superstition that this plant robbed the soil of nutrients.

Stitchwort (*Stellaria graminea*) is another foreigner of merit, but its white star-shaped flowers bloom too early for the eyes of museum visitors. Related to chickweed, which most gardeners recognize as a pest, this plant's proclivity would be a problem if it weren't inconspicuous after it flowers. On the far side of Bull Cottage, a lemon-scented daylily has taken hold, splashing cheerful yellow patches up and down the hill.

A delightful plant that finds its way into sunny garden beds and one which few have the heart to remove is the mullein (*Verbascum thapsus*). This is a roadside weed, also a biennial, which in its second year shoots up a single seven-foot stalk covered with bright yellow blossoms. It seeds itself here and there and is a welcome, if not planned, addition to gardens and pathways.

Several "garden runaways" are not as welcome as those above. One of these, goutweed (*Aegopodium podagraria*), is a pleasant-looking green-and-white variegated ground cover with white blooms in June, used with success in several well-defined museum beds. It was planted, however, on the hillside where it now promiscuously slithers in and out of the Bull Cottage garden, through areas of delicate wild flowers. Elsewhere, it bullies its way around the hillside with great self-assurance, throwing out leaves and flowers everywhere. Pulling bits of it up is useless, as any section of the underground stem left in the ground creates new roots and stems.

Left: Foxglove stands two to five feet high.

Right: Mullein is a roadside weed which in its second year shoots up a single seven-foot stalk.

The Environmental
Pavilion in October.
This is a Victorian-
style structure of
southern pine,
western fir, and
hand-split cedar.
Changing exhibits
explore environ-
mental concerns.

60

End Note: **A year on the mountain**

In the Adirondacks, the days don't move gently around the calendar year. Instead, they crackle, waft, radiate, and shudder from one month to another. The Adirondack seasons are strong, masterful, and unrelenting. No conversation among North Country people is finished without addressing today's weather—and yesterday's and tomorrow's.

Spring is not a preferred season in the mountains. It is cold, grey, and muddy. The mud oozes in tiny gullies and rivulets from melting mountain tops to crackling lakes, already groaning with splitting ice. As soon as this ice breaks up, haunting whistles and hoots resound from the water as pairs of loons lay claim to their summer nesting sites. From the muddy banks, brave green shoots emerge, struggling to unwind, unfold, and stand tall in the barely warm sunlight. An advance guard of the dreaded blackfly appears, a foreshadowing of the hungry swarms to follow. At the museum, mallards and black ducks are fetched from Ithaca for a summer of free-range paddling in the Boat Pond. Newly ordered trees, shrubs, and perennials arrive for planting. A host of flowers—trilliums, columbines, trout lilies, and stitchworts among them—bloom on Merwin Hill, too early for museum visitors, but a welcome sight for stiff, hungry insects in search of nectar. The museum's gardening crew returns and plunges into the business at hand: cleaning, raking, preparing the soil, planting, and transplanting.

As the moist soil warms and the sun arcs higher in the sky, the sharp dark lines of the forest are softened by filmy green fern fronds, wide shapely leaves of mountain maples, and shaggy rugs of moss. Summer brings on the public *persona* of the Adirondacks. Boat liveries, ice cream parlors, and lakeside motels welcome tourists. Surprisingly, summer is a moody season, being prone to days of drizzle, then days of sun, and the rainy spells bring record numbers of visitors. The parking lot, ready to receive its annual quota of 100,000 visitors, is once again full of cars, RVs, and trailers. On the grounds, care begins in earnest of the growing populations of petunias and geraniums, as well as of the View Deck annuals. In the roadside flower display, grassy tufts sprout between the roadside weeds and must be removed. Soon daisies, forget-me-nots, orange hawkweed, and buttercups are in full flower, competing well with lilies, iris, and peonies. An indigo bunting, having spent the summer south, darts by, leaving an invisible streak of blue; monarch butterflies bounce orange from flower to flower.

The favorite season of many local residents is autumn. Autumn is strong and dependable, with its hillsides flaring red and orange, and its days warm and nights crisp. The inevitable sharp frosty night in September dissolves the frivolity of summer and ushers in a glorious month of cool sunny days. Red squirrels and chipmunks scurry about, hoarding for

Visitors continue to browse the museum until mid-October. Left: Sedum flowers well into fall.

A Year on the Mountain

winter, and geese and swallows rise to the distant call of the south, as do many retired residents who prefer to spend the cold Adirondack months in a warm climate. Visitors continue to browse the museum until mid-October, admiring nature's annual exhibit of burning hills and mountains which outshines all of the museum's gardens. In concert, the barberry hedge around the Boat Bubble glows crimson, and the tamaracks become golden yellow. The "poor man's boxwood" is transplanted from the corner boxes on the View Deck to the Cutting Garden to ensure its survival, and the other flower boxes are covered on clear nights to postpone the inevitable end of the annual flowers. Asters, sedums, and roses flower well into October and then die back to recede deep into the ground until spring. Chicken wire is erected around hemlocks, cedars, and yews to forestall hungry deer, and plywood teepees are raised over tender azaleas and plants near the roof drip lines to prevent snow from crushing them.

With the first snowfall that stays (there are always several false alarms in late fall), the scene takes on a private, vast, serene dimension. Winter is the secret and the pride of year-around residents. With four to nine feet of snow a year and

temperatures plunging to thirty below, nature prevails in all things: the magic of a snowflake and the loneliness of a three-day storm; the joy of snowshoes and the anxiety of a dead battery and disappearing woodpile. The museum staff continues to plan, research, construct, and communicate, with only half an eye on the grounds. After a snowstorm, paths are plowed and broken branches removed, but for the most part, the flower beds, the wild flower trail, the ornamental plantings are on their own. Ironically, the snowier the winter, the more gloriously will the peonies and iris perform in the summer, layered as they are with a thick cover of snow. It is the trees and shrubs that take the brunt of winter, naked against the silently plunging temperature and howling northern winds, especially if a dry autumn has left the ground brittle.

From the silent, untrod museum View Deck, 24 flowerless planting boxes, perched high above the frozen lake, bide their time until spring heralds the arrival of the gardeners and the trusty John Deere cart filled with a fresh dose of compost for the next generation of seedlings. Meanwhile, invisible except inside nursery catalogs, radiantly colored marigolds and petunias wait patiently for the pages of the calendar to turn.

A view of Blue Mountain Lake in autumn.

The Adirondack
Museum and Blue
Mountain from the
air in winter.

Tributes

Eleanor Wheeler

Eleanor Wheeler grows wonderful heather. Identified with the craggy cliffs and mild, moisture-laden air of Scotland, heather is not suited to the Adirondacks, but Eleanor's are exquisite, tumbling in great pink, mauve, and purple mounds out of her woods into the sunshine. A staunch New Englander, Eleanor has a touch for gardens, plants, and life, and has served as informal guardian of the museum grounds for many years. Summer after summer, she has come by with baskets of plants, advice, and suggestions from her own garden ("my gift to the museum, in memory of Mary Hochschild"), and has been instrumental in keeping the grounds high on the list of museum priorities.

Eleanor is a transplant to the Adirondacks. After three children, a successful suburban home and garden, and a closet full of Saks Fifth Avenue dresses, Eleanor remarried and spent twenty years helping her Cornell-professor husband map the interior of Labrador. When he died suddenly, she elected to stay in the small isolated farmhouse they had just bought to retire to outside Blue Mountain Lake and had soon tamed the small clearing into flower beds, rock gardens, woodland landscapes. Her heather, Japanese primroses, perennial wild geraniums, and anemones delight Eleanor's guests as they bemoan their own sorry attempts at gardening. Eleanor has spent ninety years experiencing life's adventures and is more generous, irreverent, and curious than most of us with younger bodies. An outing with Eleanor to find the farm that grows only purple potatoes or the monks who make cheesecake and tame unruly dogs, topped by a roadside picnic of delicious cheddar and sherry, is a day remembered.

Jim Cooney

It is an army of only two, but it is formidable. In the small commandeered John Deere vehicle, Jim, armed with Felco pruning shears, and Charlie Sprauer, his assistant, ornamented with red suspenders, stage a number of daily battles with unruly shrubs and weeds, hungry flowers, and hungrier insects. They make up the museum's present gardening staff, a camaraderie preceded by several sturdy, hardworking gardeners such as Ken Cornwall, a lover of flowers, and his son, Scott, who succeeded him, and whose wife, Mary, still works at the museum.

Jim Cooney is a professional nurseryman. For many years, while he worked at NL Industries, the mine at Tahawus, he ran a small greenhouse nursery in Long Lake just north of Blue Mountain Lake and provided annuals to summer-starved locals, including the museum staff. Four years ago, after fifteen years of work with the museum, he became the museum's gardener and now his work borders on legendary. One tale started the day Jim appeared in his pickup truck with a massive tree trunk riddled with peeling bark and insect holes. Other workers watched as he wrestled the trunk to the side of the nature trail on Merwin Hill, positioned it carefully, and planted some ferns in it. "We spend all our time hauling debris *out* of the museum—and Jim brings it back!" It was worse when he dug up a patch of beautiful Kentucky bluegrass, hauled in gritty sand, and planted it with scruffy clover, hawkweed and mullein. He was creating one of the naturalized exhibits, the Roadside Flowers, which still looks as scruffy today (as it should).

Jim is responsible to a demanding and sometimes fickle timetable. Chores involving petunias and geraniums are completely predictable: daily checking, weekly pinching (the spent flowers), biweekly fertilizing. Other chores are periodic, like reminding the maintenance crew to pay attention to the cardinal flowers when they clean the drainage ditch with the front-end loader. Still others are unpredictable: whether or not to move the beautiful hard-to-grow maidenhair from the area reserved for

Tributes

bunchberries; whether to try white trilliums in the native garden though they need more alkaline soil; whether to re-stake the lilies only to have the deer trample them once more.

Alone in his sensitivity and know-how with plants, and with the help of the strong-backed and ready-to-work Charlie, Jim daily maneuvers through the obstacle course of nature's demands, whims, and secrets.

Craig Gilborn

The museum opens to visitors at 9:30 in the morning. The offices open at 9:00. And Craig Gilborn walks at 8:00. Since he came to the Adirondack Museum from Wilmington, Delaware, Craig has roamed the misty campus in early morning, usually with the family dog. Director of the Adirondack Museum and resident for twenty years, since 1972 Craig has nurtured ongoing exhibits and nudged new ones into existence. Trained in early American culture at the H. F. DuPont Winterthur Museum, which itself hosts exquisite gardens, he has a surprisingly strong interest in plants, an interest manifested both personally and professionally.

Professionally, Craig has not only kept the original garden planted by Mary Hochschild healthy and true by allocating proper attention and funding (not common for a history museum), but he has also expanded it physically and spiritually. The museum was originally founded to plot the exploration, settlement, and subsequent relationship of humans to the Adirondacks. A small portrait of alpine plants within the mountain-climbing paraphernalia and of trees in the logging exhibit were among the few displays describing nature's role. Craig began to turn this around, both because the environment was becoming increasingly fragile, and because people were concerned and interested. In 1987, the natural setting of Merwin Hill became a nature-filled exhibit in itself, and, now, an exhibit bounded by woods, boulders, and a pond is being developed to give visitors the chance to experience the forest from a marked trail.

Personally, Craig's commitment to the gardens is reflected in his own gardening efforts. In late winter, he buys flats, soil, and seeds, sets up a potting shed on his sun porch, and starts some of the annual flowers that will spend the summer in the museum's cutting garden.

The best of Craig's flowers, however, are those summer visitors will never see—the bulbs he plants in October, stores in a cool museum basement for several months, and retrieves to exhibit on the Gilborns' dining table in March. Through the window, behind the brave colorful bursts of narcissus, tulips, and hyacinths, snow swirls across the frozen lake and mountains beyond. For Craig and gardeners everywhere, these blossoms are the hope of what is to come.

Index

Aaron's rod (*Thermopsis
caroliniana*) 22, 23, 32
Ageratum 28
Amsonia (*Amsonia
tabernaemontana*) 23, 32
Anemone 68
Arrowwood (*Viburnum dentatum*)
37
Ash 31
Ash, mountain (*Sorbus
americana*) **9**, 43
Aster 31, 64
Astilbe 16, 23, 38
Azalea, 14, 26, 36, 64
Azalea, Exbury 'Aurora' 37
Azalea, pinkster (*Rhododendron
periclymenoides*) 36

Baby's-breath (*Gypsophila
paniculata*) **19**, 20, 22, 23, 26, **49**
Balloon flower (*Platycodon
grandiflorus*) 18, **19**, 38
Balsam (*Abies balsamea*) 23, 40,
42, 55
Barberry 64

Bee balm (*Monarda didyma
'Croftway Pink'*) **21**, 23, 32
Beech (*Fagus grandifolia*) 31, 49
Begonia 28, **29**
Bergenia (*Bergenia cordifolia*) 14,
26, 55
Birch, white (*Betula papyrifera*)
23, 31, 42, 43, 49
Black-eyed Susan (*Rudbeckia
hirta*) 32, **50**, 51
Bleeding heart 26, 54
Blueberry bush 23, 36
Bluegrass, Kentucky 69
Boxwood, poor man's (*Teucrium
chamaedrys*) 30, 44, 64
Bunchberry (*Cornus canadensis*)
50, 70
Burning bush (*Euonymus alata
'Compacta'*) 36
Buttercup 22, 26, 32, 63
Butterfly weed (*Asclepias
tuberosa*) 20, 32

Cardinal flower 14, 48
Cattail 22
Cedar, northern white (*Thuja
occidentalis*) 40, **43**
Cedar, red (*Juniperus virginiana*)
20

Cereus, night-blooming 18
Chickweed 59
Chicory (*Cichorium intybus*) 38,
51
Chive 55
Cinquefoil, bush (*Potentilla
fruticosa*) 16, 23, 26, 32, 34,
35, 38
Clover 69
Cohosh, black (*Cimicifuga
racemosa*) 23
Cohosh, blue-berried
(*Caulophyllum thalictroides*) 50
Colt's-foot (*Tussilago farfara*) 26,
50
Columbine, native 26, 48, 62
Comfrey 55
Coral bell (*Heuchera sanguinea*)
13, 18, 23, **26**, **27**
Cornflower (*Centaurea montana*)
20
Cranberry 36
Crocus (*Crocus nudiflorus*) 24, 44

Dahlia **31**
Daisy, common (*Chrysanthemum
leucanthemum*) **31**, 32, 51, 63
Daisy, shasta (*Chrysanthemum
maximum*) 20, 38, **49**

Dawn redwood (*Metasequoia glyptostroboides*) 12
Daylily (*Hemerocallis*) **11**, 16, 20, **21**, 22, 23, 32, 38, **46**, **55**, 59
Delphinium, blue **14**, **19**, 20, 23, 32
Doll's-eyes (*Actaea pachypoda*) 44, 50
Dwarf baby's-breath (*Gypsophila repens*) 23
Dwarf dahlia 28
Dwarf highbush cranberry (*Viburnum trilobum var. nana*) 36
Elderberry bush 11

Fern, bracken (*Pteridium aquilinum*) 51
Fern, cinnamon (*Osmunda cinnamomea*) 24
Fern, interrupted (*O. claytoniana*) 24
Fern, lady 51
Fern, maidenhair (*Adiantum pedatum*) 51, 69
Fern, New York 51
Fern, rock (*Polypodium vulgare*) 51
Fern, royal (*O. regalis*) **24**

Fern, wood 51
Fir, Algerian 12
Fir, Spanish 12
Forget-me-not, blue (*Myosotis scorpioides*) 26, 50, 63
Foxglove (*Digitalis purpurea*) **11**, 16, 26, **58**

Gazania **8**, 28
Geranium, annual, 12, 63, 69
Geranium, wild 55, 68
Goldenrod 44, 48, 58
Goldthread (*Coptis trifolia*) 50
Goutweed (*Aegopodium podagraria*) 26, 59

Hawkweed, orange (*Hieracium aurantiacum*) 32, **47**, 51, 63, 69
Heather 68
Heliopsis (*Heliopsis helianthoides*) 16, 22, 44
Hemlock (*Tsuga canadensis*) 23, 40, 42, 43
Highbush cranberry (*Viburnum trilobum*) 36, **37**
Hills-of-snow (*Hydrangea arborescens* 'Grandiflora') 34, 38
Holly 37

Hosta 16, 24, 32, 55
Hyacinth 71
Hydrangea (*Hydrangea arborescens* 'Grandiflora') 34, 38
Hydrangea, peegee (*Hydrangea paniculata* 'Grandiflora') 18, 20, 34, 44
Hydrangea shrubs 16, 32, **34**, **54**, 55

Impatiens 28, 31
Iris, bearded 16, 18, **20**, 22, 26, 63, 64
Iris, Siberian (*Iris sibirica*) 16, **18**, **19**, **20**, 22, 23, 32

Jack-in-the-pulpit (*Arisaema triphyllum*) 50
Juniper, creeping (*Juniperus horizontalis* 'Blue Rug') 20

Labrador-tea (*Ledum groenlandicum* Oeder) 23
Lady's-slipper, pink (*Cypripedium acaule*) 26, 50
Lambs'-ears (*Stachys lanata* or *S. byzantina*) 38, 55
Larch (*Larix laricina*) 42, 64

Index

Lavender 55
Lettuce, wild 48
Lichen, red-topped or 'British soldiers' 51
Ligularia (*Ligularia sibirica*) 55
Lilac 14, 16, 36
Lily 13, 23, 32, 38, 55, 63, 70
Lily, bluebead (*Clintonia borealis*) 50
Lily, Turk's-cap (*Lilium superbum*) 15, 38, 44, **52**
Liverwort 48, 51
Lobelia 28
Locust, black (*Robinia pseudoacacia*) **16**, **17**, 26, 43
Loosestrife 23
Lungwort (*Pulmonaria officinalis*) 26, 55
Lupine, Carolina (*Thermopsis caroliniana*) 22
Lupine, pink 14, **15**
Lupine, spiky 26, 59

Magnolia 6, 12
Maple 11, 42, 43

Maple, mountain (*Acer spicatum*) 49, 63
Maple, red 46
Maple, striped (*Acer pensylvanicum*) 49
Maple, sugar (*Acer saccharum*) 36, **41**, 42
Marigold **26**, **27**, **28**, 64
Marsh mallow 48
Meadow rue (*Thalictrum polygamum*) 32, 50
Meadowsweet (*Spiraea latifolia*) 32, 37
Mock-orange (*Philadelphus coronarius*) 14, 23, 26, 36
Moss 48, 51, 63
Moss, club 51
Moss, sphagnum 43
Mountain ash (*Sorbus americana*) **11**, 43
Mullein (*Verbascum thapsus*) 32, **46**, **59**, 69
Myrtle (*Vinca minor*) 16, 18, 26, 46, 58

Narcissus 71

Oat, wild 48, 58

Orchid, purple fringed (*Habenaria fimbriata* or *H. psycodes var. grandiflora*) 50
Oregon grape (*Mahonia aquifolium*) 14, **15**, 54
Osier, red (*Cornus stolonifera* or *C. sericea*) 50
Osmunda ferns 24

Parsley 54
Peegee hydrangea (*Hydrangea paniculata* 'Grandiflora') 18, 20, 34
Peony (*Paeonia lactiflora*) **13**, **20**, 22, 26, 55, 63, 64
Petunia **12**, 30, 54, 63, 64, 69
Phlox (*Phlox paniculata*) 16, 20, 22, **23**, 32, 38
Pine, white (*Pinus strobus*) 23, 40, 42, 49
Pitcher-plant (*Sarracenia purpurea*) 23
Plantain weed 31
Poor man's boxwood (*Teucrium chamaedrys*) 33, 44, 64
Poplar 13
Poplar, balsam (*Populus balsamifera*) **38**, **39**, **41**, 43
Poplar, white (*Populus alba*) 43

Portulaca 28
Potentilla 18
Primrose, Japanese 68

Queen Anne's lace **47**

Rhododendron 14
Rhododendron periclymenoides
36
Rhubarb 55
Rose 14, 44, **55**, 64
Rose (*Rosa rugosa*) 32, 37, 38

Sage 55
Salvia 28
Sedum 30, 44, **62**, 64
Solomon's plume (*Smilacina
racemosa*) 26, **47**, 50
Solomon's-seal (*Polygonatum
pubescens*) 26, 50
Spiderwort (*Tradescantia x.
Andersoniana*) 23, 32
Spruce, black (*Picea mariana*) 53
Spruce, red (*Picea rubens*) 23, 40
Spruce, white (*Picea glauca*) 42
St. Johnswort **46**
Stitchwort (*Stellaria graminea*) 26,
59, 62

Stonecrop (*Sedum spectabile*) 22
Sweet William (*Dianthus
barbatus*) 26, 58
Sweet alyssum 28
Sweet pepper (*Clethra alnifolia*)
23, 44
Syringa 36

Tamarack (*Larix laricina*) **41**, 42,
43, 64
Tarragon 55
Tartarian honeysuckle 18
Thistle, globe (*Echinops ritro*) 22,
23, 38
Tobacco plant **44, 45**
Trillium 26, 62
Trillium, painted (*Trillium
undulatum*) 49
Trillium, stinking Benjamin
(*Trillium erectum*) 49
Trillium, white 70
Trout lily (*Erythronium
americanum*) 26, 49, 62
Tulip 71
Turtle-head (*Chelone glabra*) 38,
50

Veronica latifolia 'Icicle' 18, **26**,
27, 54

Viburnum 36, 37
Virgin's-bower (*Clematis
virginiana*) 38, 51
Virginia creeper (*Parthenocissus
quinquefolia*) 59

Waterlily 58
Willow 43
Winterberry (*Ilex verticillata*) 37
Wintergreen (*Pyrola chlorantha*)
50
Witch-hobble (*Viburnum
alnifolium*) 37

Yarrow (*Anchillea millefolium*) **19**,
20, 32, **49**, 51
Yellowood, Kentucky (*Cladrastis
lutea*) 26, 43

During the twenty years he has lived at the Adirondack Museum, Craig Gilborn has walked the museum grounds with camera in hand, as he has watched the seasons turn. Some of the best results are on these pages.

After graduating from the University of Wisconsin at Madison, Mea Kaemmerlen was trained in horticulture at the New York Botanical Garden in New York City. She has worked as a gardener for private and public institutions and has written extensively on gardens. An aching back has now limited her horticultural activity to a personal herb garden, some consulting, and some writing. To support these indulgences, she works as director of publications at International Schools Services in Princeton, New Jersey.